Presented to

_____

by

_____

Date

_____

A
Month
of
Meditations
for
MOTHERS

DIMENSIONS
FOR LIVING
NASHVILLE

Library of Congress Cataloging-in-Publication Data

Carcaño, Minerva Garza.
    A month of meditations for mothers / Minerva Garza Carcaño, Leanne H. Ciampa, Helen Hempfling Enari.
        p. cm.
    ISBN 0-687-09940-4 (alk. paper)
    1. Mothers—Prayer-books and devotions—English. 2. Parenting—Religious aspects—Christianity—Meditations. 3. Devotional calendars. I. Ciampa, Leanne Hensley, 1961-.   . II. Enari, Helen Hempfling. III. Title.
    BV4529.18 .C37 2000
    242'.6431—dc21

00-060226

Unless otherwise noted, Scripture quotations are from the *New Revised Standard Version of the Bible*, copyright 1989, Division of Christian Education of the National Council of the Churches of Christ in the United States of America. Used by permission. All rights reserved.

Meditations in this book were compiled from *365 Meditations for Mothers of Young Children*, copyright © 1993 by Dimensions for Living. Reprinted by permission.

Meditations 2, 8, 12, 14, 15, and 17 were written by Minerva Garza Carcaño. Meditations 1, 5, 6, 7, 9, 13, 21, 23, 25, and 31 were written by Leanne H. Ciampa. Meditations 10, 11, 19, 22, 24, 28, and 29 were written by Helen Hempfling Enari. Meditations 3, 16, 18, 27, and 30 were written by Margaret Anne Huffman. Meditations 4, 20, and 26 were written by Sheron C. Patterson.

00 01 02 03 04 05 06 07 08 09—10 9 8 7 6 5 4 3 2 1

MANUFACTURED IN THE UNITED STATES OF AMERICA

1

Meditate on John 14:1-3.

Sometimes I look at my children and think, *What would you do without me?* I feed them, bathe them, and give them shelter and security. They often seem so strong, so able to do for themselves, but still they are babies needing their mother's love. And they never question that love. They know that if they need food, I will get it for them; or if they need a blanket on a cold night, I will get it for them. There is no need that, if I am able, I will not provide for them.

That is what Jesus was talking about when he promised to always care for us. He promised to go prepare a place for us and return to take us there. And we, like children depending on our mothers, can depend on his words. For Christ will provide all that we need, not only for this life but also for our life eternal.

O God, thank you for providing all the warmth, love, and security we will ever need. I look forward with confidence to my life and the lives of my children that will be spent in eternity with you.

———

2

Meditate on Psalm 40:1-3.

Before my daughter was born I suffered two miscarriages. They were both difficult experiences, but during the second miscarriage God touched my life in a transforming way.

It was Christmas Eve, a day of life and hope, but Thomas and I were again facing death; dying was our hope of a child, our dreams of a family, our desire to pass on our humble legacies.

It was a cold day. The hospital was dark and empty. It seemed as if patients and staff had all gone home. We felt alone and abandoned. We knew exactly what was happening to us and that there was nothing that we could do about it except pray.

Eventually I was left alone in a sterile and unfriendly operating room, and I prayed even more telling God that I could not go further without his help. Then I heard a voice. I did not recognize the voice, but the person to whom the voice belonged seemed to know me. As she came within my range of vision, I realized that it was a Christian friend whom I knew. She was to be the nurse assisting through the surgical procedure that I would have to undergo. She took my hand and told me how much she appreciated me. I felt comforted as my body gave in to the anesthesia.

As I came through the procedure, I heard another voice; and again though I did not recognize the voice, the person spoke to me with familiarity. She was telling me that she was changing my gown so that I would feel more comfortable. As I began to see more clearly, I recognized her. She was another Christian friend, whose children I had come to know well through church. She shared with me how much her children loved me. Then she told me that she and the other friend who had been with me earlier had not been scheduled to work that day, but early that morning they had both been called to come into work.

My prayers had begun very early that morning. Some would say, "What a coincidence that these friends would be there for you." But I say that God is faithfully present in our lives and responds to our prayers when we call out to him. With the psalmist I will praise God!

Dear God, I am so thankful for your faithful and loving presence in my life. As I face the challenges of motherhood that lie ahead, I am encouraged and strengthened by the knowledge that you hear my every prayer.

3

Meditate on Psalm 118:24.

It was a dank basement room behind the belching furnace, but it took paint and dehumidifying fairly well. I set up a sandbox and picnic table and called it a playroom. It was not the best playroom, but the tired, financially strapped mind takes what is available.

The kids loved it.

On rainy days, we played there, taking off on jaunts of imagination, up, up, and away to lofty tree houses aboard rainbow railroads.

And on Sundays, we dined on my finest china—never mind that the oldest child was not yet through first grade, the youngest not yet through diapers. They were careful; I was attentive as our best selves were reflected in polished goblets. Candles stood tall in homemade juice-can candelabra; cloth napkins mopped up drippy chins.

We communed over baked beans and hot dogs, animal crackers and chocolate milk. Love, when taken in and passed around our rickety picnic table, was a transforming moment, as all gatherings around the family table can be.

Lord, show us where the bright spots wait for us to find them in the chaotic days of mothering. Help us pull them from behind furnaces, frowns, sad days, scary days, lonely days. May we remember to enjoy the "best china" moments now, rather than saving them for later; regret for having missed opportunities for celebrating the bright spots of life would make a bitter dessert in years to come.

Meditate on Isaiah 64:8.

Looking through some of our wedding photos, I hardly recognize myself. Something has changed me; I don't know the old me anymore. We aren't alike at all. We talk differently, think differently, and even walk differently.

I am different now because I am a mother. The very existence of my child makes me somebody else. Because he is my son, I am a mother; because he needs food and drink, I am a provider; because he needs to learn, I am a teacher; because he thrives on security and love, I am a nurturer.

I am happy because he is happy, and I realize that my capacity to be all that I am comes from God. God enables me to be a mother with all the trimmings.

Dear God, I am somebody new. I am a mother. Motherhood is one of the greatest events in my life. You shape and mold me so that I can handle the job, as though I am clay on the potter's wheel. Keep your hands on me.

5

Meditate on Matthew 5:14-16.

My children, like many children, will not go to bed unless their night-light is on. The thing that tickles me about the night-light, however, is that it really doesn't put out much light. For all intents and purposes, after I turn it on, the room is still dark. But in my children's eyes, that night-light makes a very dark, frightening room a cozy, safe place to sleep.

That little night-light has changed the way I see my role as a Christian in this world. I used to hear Christ's words about "letting my light shine" and feel really overwhelmed, thinking I would have to be a really outstanding Christian to even be seen in this dark world of ours. Drugs, violence, racial hatred, poverty—darkness is everywhere we look. And somehow Christ wants me to shine, to overcome the darkness. It seemed impossible until I thought about that little night-light.

I may not be the best Christian in the world, but

I try my hardest to shine. And just like that tiny night-light in my children's room, my light may be all someone needs to feel safe and cozy in this scary, dark world. So like the night-light, I'll keep on shining.

O God, let your light shine through me, and may I, like the light that brings so much comfort to my children, bring comfort and hope to others.

6

Meditate on Psalm 98.

A few weeks ago I arrived to pick up my boys after Sunday school, and my four-year-old came running to me, saying, "Listen to what I learned to do!" Then he let out the most blood-curdling scream I have ever heard as he clapped his hands. I thought, *Oh, my! Has he been yelling the entire time he has been here? They are going to tell me never to bring him back again!*

By now, both my children were screaming and clapping their hands. Then my four-year-old said, "Come on, Mom, make a joyful noise to the Lord like we are!" Not wanting to do it, I said, "I don't know how." My son replied, "Well, I just think about God, and all this happiness pops out!"

Suddenly I didn't care if he had been screaming the entire time; he had learned a Bible verse I hope he always remembers: "Make a joyful noise to the Lord" (Psalm 98:4*a*). To me, and perhaps to God, those embarrassing screams suddenly became songs of praise!

O God, your presence makes such a difference in my children's lives. Help me find that same joy in my life. I want to think of your name and let the joy "pop out," for because of you I have many things to sing and shout and clap about.

———

7

Meditate on Luke 12:6-7.

My son recently had to have his tonsils taken out. He and I had been sitting in a hospital room for some time. It was just he and I, since I am a single parent and my mother and father were keeping my other son. We sat there for a long time, just the two of us, talking about the things that would happen next. I tried to do the best job I could of preparing him for his surgery.

Finally the time came, and he was put on a cart and whisked off to surgery. I thought I was prepared for the moment, but my heart sank when they wheeled his cart away from me. My baby was going off to a new experience, and I could not go with him. It didn't seem right. I was there when he learned to take his first steps, when he learned to say his first words, and when he learned to pedal his tricycle. I should be with him now! I knew he was afraid, and he looked so tiny and helpless as they rolled him into the operating room.

I wanted to yell, "Stop! Forget it! Just give him to me, and I will take him home." I wanted to jump on that cart and go with him into the operating room. I wanted to cry. I wanted to be strong. And then the words of Jesus suddenly came to me: "Even the hairs on your head are counted." I thought, "God, you know every hair on my little boy's head. I can't go with him into that operating room, but you can." I let my son go, and I felt better knowing that God went with him.

O God, if I could, I'd go with my children through every difficult experience they will ever have. I won't always be there when they need help and guidance, but you will. You know and love my children even better than I do. So when I can't be there, when I can't help them, thank you for being with them.

8

Meditate on Job 1:20-21.

Can anyone be more important in a child's life than his or her mother? As mothers, we would undoubtedly answer No, no one is more important to a child than his or her mother. Job disagrees with us. Even more important than us is the Lord, from whom our children came and to whom they return.

I spend time with my child, attempting to develop a relationship between her and me that I hope will be loving, affirming, challenging, joyous, and special. This is an important part of mothering. I am sure that you do the same. But just as it is important that we take time to develop such a relationship with our children, it is also important that we guide them in building a strong and solid relationship with God, their Creator.

Our children's first and last relationship is not with us but with God. Their relationship with God will be the one constant in their lives. As they grow, they will determine whether they will be close or distant in this relationship, but God has promised that he will always be present for them. At some moments, God's presence in their lives may be one of judgment. At other moments it may be one of mercy. Always the divine presence will be grace-filled.

As much as I may work on my relationship with my daughter, Sofía Teresa, I recognize that I am but a finite and imperfect being. God, and God alone, will always be there for her in the most perfect of ways. For this reason, I want her to know God throughout her life.

God, from whom we come and to whom we return, you alone are always with us. In birth and in death you accompany us. In your mercy and in your love, reveal yourself to our children. Care for them and receive them in your own good time.

9

Meditate on Deuteronomy 5:16.

It wasn't until I had my own baby that I knew just how much my mother loved me. I looked into his eyes and realized how much love a mother is capable of feeling.

It wasn't until he talked back to me and said "I hate you" for the first time that I knew how much a child's words can hurt a mother. I thought I would burst into tears at that very moment.

A mother's love is a precious thing—so strong, so constant. But a mother's heart is a fragile thing, breaking at even the smallest hurt.

O God, I wish I had listened more closely to your commandment and honored my mother more constantly. So many things I did and said I wish I could take back. Now that I am a mother, may I treat my children with love and respect so that honoring me is an easier task.

Meditate on Colossians 3:13.

I said something that hurt Sam's feelings. It wasn't intentional, but he was right to be upset. He came to me trying to hold back his tears. "You hurt my feelings," he said as tears spilled out of his big brown eyes. Then he hugged me, crawled onto my lap, cuddled, and continued to cry as I told him over and over again how sorry I was. Within ten minutes he was feeling better. He looked up at me with a smile and said, "That's okay, Mommy. I still love you." Then he ran off to play.

What a lesson in forgiveness! If we adults could do what Sam was able to do, we would be much healthier and happier people. As adults, we tend to deal with our hurt and anger in unhealthy ways. We hide our feelings. We avoid the one who has hurt us. We want to hurt the one who first hurt us. We are unable to forgive freely and fully. We are unable to go on with our lives.

Instead of running away in anger, Sam took the initiative to confront me with what I had said. Instead of holding me at arm's length until I apologized, he crawled right up into my lap. Instead of ignoring or avoiding me, he hugged me. Instead of holding in his feelings, he cried. And when he felt that his anger had been heard, he was able to forgive and go on with his life.

Gracious God, help me to forgive.

———

11

Meditate on Psalm 19:1.

I have a collection of the most beautiful rocks in the world. Never mind that most of them are pieces of gravel found in alleys and driveways. Never mind that a good many more are small red lava stones used to landscape neighbors' gardens. They are still the most beautiful rocks in the world. They are my son's favorite rocks, chosen carefully and given with love. To him, each rock he gives me is unique and special. He keeps track of them and becomes greatly offended when he catches me weeding my rock collection.

What a gift it is to be able to see value and beauty in the most ordinary things! Yet, if we think about it, there is nothing that is ordinary about God's creation. Each part of God's creation has its own unique beauty. When we look at our surroundings through the eyes of a happy and curious child, the world becomes an amazing place—a place where acorns are transformed into diamonds and ladybugs take on their own personalities, where swing sets become ships and pine trees become castles, where full moons become vanilla cookies and crescent moons become bananas. The world is, indeed, a marvelous place.

God, help me marvel at the beauty that surrounds me every day.

———

12

Meditate on Psalm 104.

The day that Thomas and I brought our firstborn home was a somewhat scary day. We were "old folks" in comparison to most new parents—I was thirty-seven and Thomas was forty—and we were setting out on a new venture. What would we do with this tiny bundle of person in our hands? Would we know when to feed her and how to take care of her? Would we know when she was ill and know what to do? How would we help her grow? Would we know how to discipline her? What would we teach her? We were nervous.

To make matters worse, our daughter just cried and cried and cried as we attempted to sign all the papers that the hospital needed for our dismissal. She did not want to be nursed. She did not want to be carried, but neither did she want to be put in her bassinet. The attendant who pushed my wheelchair out of the hospital suggested I stick a finger in the baby's mouth to stop her crying. Our daughter was getting on *her* nerves, too! But then something happened—something that made me aware of the fact that whatever I might be able to teach this child, this gift of God, there would be many things that she would teach me as well.

Though our baby had been crying for what seemed a solid hour, the minute we stepped outside the hospital she immediately stopped crying. I had just covered her with a light blanket and was watching her take a deep breath, her eyes opening wide as she felt the breeze on her cheek. Not only did she stop crying, but she also became very still. Only her eyes moved as we passed under the trees at the entrance to the hospital. She seemed aware of the fact that she was coming into contact with something new and wonderful. As the sun hit her brow she squinted her eyes, and I thought that I saw her trying to open them ever so slightly as she became accustomed to the sunlight.

Watching her made me aware of that beautiful day. I realized as I followed her movements and expressions that she was indeed seeing God's creation for the very first time in her life. Birds were chirping. Could she hear the birds? I wondered. People were coming and going. Could she sense their presence? Could she smell the fresh air? It was an amazing experience to observe her encounter with God's handiwork.

Even more amazing was, through her help, to have my old eyes see God's creation in a new way. I learned a significant lesson from my then three-day-old daughter. God's creation is marvelous and wonderful, filled with beauty and grand surprises, if only we'll stop to see it and hear it and feel it. The psalmist must have had this freshness of spirit when he wrote Psalm 104.

Our children have so much to teach us about God's creation. During this day may we be their attentive students, seeing life through their eyes and allowing our spirits to be renewed by their witness.

Dear God, for our children who help us to know you in new ways, we give you thanks.

13

Meditate on Deuteronomy 6:4-9.

Whenever I see a yellow school bus, I wonder what it will be like to put my children on one and send them to school to learn how to read and write and add and subtract. I am glad my children will have trained teachers, for I am not sure I could teach them these things.

My children will learn many things at school, but there is much they will not learn there. They will not learn about God or Jesus or the greatest commandment or how to pray. No, I will be their primary teacher in these things. At times I feel unsure about my qualifications for the job, but I know that God will guide me and remind me of the importance of this task.

O God, help me teach my children your ways. Help me tell them stories of you and your Son and the Holy Spirit that they will understand

and love. And, above all, I pray that my actions and words will teach them about faith and joy and the peace that comes from knowing you.

———

14

Meditate on Judges 5:1-7.

So often when we think of mothering, our thoughts are of small children and lullabies. Some of us may think of car pools and day care. Others of us may think of the jobs of being breadwinners and perhaps sole supporters of families. Usually we tend to think of mothering in the context of our immediate families. The prophetess and judge Deborah, however, gives us another model.

In her wisdom, Deborah arose to be a mother for all of Israel. When Deborah's people found themselves under the tyranny of captivity, it was she who laid out the battle plan, even choosing and commissioning and accompanying the troops into battle. Through Deborah, God brought salvation to his people.

I believe there are women among us today who are being called by God not only to be mothers within our own family circles but also to be spiritual mothers in our communities of faith and wise and courageous mothers for a hurting world—mothers in the footsteps of those such as Deborah, Joan of Arc, Susan Anthony, Rosa Parks, Harriet Tubman, or Mother Teresa. Women who have, through their womanhood, talents, and love, mothered society for the better. Might God be calling you to enlarge your vision of the realm where your gifts of mothering may be needed?

God of all wisdom, help us discern your call for our lives. In all things, enable us to be mothers of hope and healing.

15

Meditate on Matthew 6:33.

I grew up next door to my maternal grandparents, and as a child I did everything that I could to spend as much time at their house as possible. There was good reason for this. My grandparents' home was always bustling with activity: constant visits from aunts, uncles, and cousins; interesting conversations; and always plenty of food, regardless of the hour of day. There would often be new relatives to meet from just down the road or from as far as remote villages in Mexico. I was amazed at how large our family was and how wealthy my grandparents were to host such splendid meals for those who came to visit.

It was not until some years later that I discovered that all those aunts, uncles, and cousins were not all relatives in the strict sense of the word. I also came to know that by the standards of the community we lived in, my grandparents and our entire family were poor. Many of the persons whom I had grown up considering relatives were actually persons whom my grandfather had met while he and his sons worked in the fields, persons whom he'd encountered along dusty country roads, or persons he'd heard about from others. They were persons who had had some need in their lives when my grandfather had met them, and my grandfather had extended a helping hand to them, welcomed them into his home, and shared his family's food with them. As I now recall, the meals that I'd participated in were actually simple meals of beans, fried potatoes, tortillas, and other such foods. They were nothing close to fine meals, but in their spirit and in their joy they were true banquets served up lovingly by my grandmother.

One day, as I was attempting to comprehend why my grandparents would open up their home in such a way to sometimes absolute strangers, and why they would give their food away to them, I heard my grandmother say, "Dios no permite que hagamos menos"—God requires no less of us.

Through these blessed grandparents of mine I first came to know the meaning of seeking first the kingdom of God and his righteousness. All other things did come as promised. Today I thank God for my grandparents.

Dear God, thank you for the gift of grandparents and the beautiful ways they bless our children's lives. Through the years may our children come to understand and appreciate those blessings seen and unseen.

16

Meditate on Genesis 1:26.

Spring arrived depressingly damp, and the children moaned at the rain-streaked windows.

The youngest, however, loved it. Raindrops for her face, puddles for her feet, and wriggle worms to adore.

She met the worms face to face, lying flat on her belly on the sidewalk, entranced that, without feet, they still arrived at their destinations, a little dried out but triumphant.

"Wigglings," she named them.

One of the neighborhood naughties, however, taught her to stomp them. Few creatures seem lowlier than worms, but they fit neatly into the eco-scheme of things, and I was horrified. Kitties, hamsters, even turtles rate backyard funerals. They also can scratch, hiss, bite, and show their displeasure at mistreatment. But worms? Nonetheless, they do warrant rescue.

"Let's help him instead," I suggested, interrupting her raised-foot aim at an unwary worm.

We nudged him onto a leaf that she carefully carried to the garden. "Here he can help our green bean seeds grow," I explained. Clapping as he inched away into the furrows, she nodded in understanding. Lots of worms were helped that afternoon, whether they needed it or not.

Lord, how quickly we learn pride in our destructive power. A raised foot to stomp worms can quickly become a raised voice or a raised hand, ready to do harm to a fellow human being. Remind us, Lord, to teach our children by example to honor each part of your creation as lovingly as you do.

40

17

Meditate on 1 John 4:11-13.

When I was a kid, I was skinny and lanky, and I had an uncle who ribbed me constantly about my appearance. "You're the strangest-looking kid I know," he would say. "Look at those arms and those long, skinny legs. . . . You look just like a mosquito!" I would look at myself in the mirror, and sure enough I did resemble a mosquito.

One morning my grandmother caught me looking at myself in the mirror with disgust and asked me if something was wrong. I told her that I hated the way that I looked and that my uncle was right—I looked just like a mosquito. She gently came over and asked me if I knew who had made me. "God," I responded, a bit perturbed that she would want to give me a Bible lesson at a moment when my entire future development was in question. She continued, "God made you, and inside you God put beauty and love. You worry about the outside, but if you look inside you will see God's beauty and love. Look in the mirror again, and don't look away until you see that beauty and love. Look way deep down inside of you."

I sat in front of that mirror for a while and contemplated her words, and then an assurance filled me. I thought at that time that it was my grandmother's wisdom and care. I now know that it was God's affirming Spirit at work in my life. I had come face to face with God's love within me.

How are your children feeling about themselves these days? Perhaps it's time to remind them that God made them with beauty and love.

Lord, help us show our children how beautifully you have made them—inside and out.

18

Meditate on Psalm 23:1-3*a*.

Kids play on teeter-totters; mothers live on them. Up and down in perpetual motion, I moved before dawn's first light, usually attending to some child or another—teeth, dreams, fevers, excitement for a new day.

Life was so different before children. Then I *"knew"* what working full-time was. After children, working full-time no longer meant forty-hour weeks; it meant perpetual vigilance, even at night.

Sometimes I liked being a mother; other times, I was not so sure, for I didn't seem to make a difference in the lives of children who rejected my meals, ignored my directives, and displayed appallingly lazy habits despite my best interventions, leaving my self-confidence in shreds.

I thought the parenting payoff would be different—a more even pace, a lighter toll on my self-esteem, and more sleep. Ha! And I never imagined just how far down the swoop of the teeter-totter would take me—or how high.

Lows and highs. One cannot exist without the other, and it was at that pivotal point of balance where the children and I met for a brief moment powerful enough to get me going again.

Lord, level us off from the extremes of mothering with reassurance that to be ambivalent is neither unreasonable nor unforgivable. Help us keep the teeter-totter moving between false highs and inaccurate lows. Tiredness slows our movement. Restore us, Lord, to green pastures where we can lie down by still waters, at least for five minutes.

———

19

Meditate on Matthew 11:28.

There is something special about a mother's kiss that makes "owies" go away. My children come to me screaming in pain, showing me where they bumped their heads or where they scraped their knees or where they stubbed their toes. I take them in my arms, tell them how sorry I am that they are hurt, and gently kiss the exact spot that is causing them so much pain. And with that kiss, their tears immediately dry up, a smile replaces the frown, and they run off to play, completely cured.

As mothers, we often see ourselves as the primary caregivers and nurturers in the family. Because of this, it is often difficult for us to allow another to take care of us when we are hurt. Although many of our own "owies" can't be healed as easily or as quickly as our children's, our hurts can be healed if we allow ourselves to be vulnerable to God's nurturing power.

Throughout the Bible, God promises to be with us, to nurture us, to sustain us, and to protect us. The Psalms are filled with words of comfort and assurance. The Beatitudes can be a source of great comfort. Many of Paul's writings affirm God's constant and nurturing presence in our lives. It is important that we know where to look when we are in need of comfort.

God, you are our great Nurturer. Help me bring my hurts to you so that I can experience the healing comfort of your embracing arms.

20

Meditate on Psalm 9:1.

Robby has an attitude of gratitude. He has learned to say a blessing over every meal. His Sunday school teacher teaches the class a new blessing every week, and he shares them at home in a piecemeal fashion that makes it hard to tell one from another.

It does not matter to me that he jumbles his words together and combines the various blessings in a mismatched way. I'm just glad he knows he is supposed to be grateful to God. I'm glad he knows that God has given him everything that he has.

Unlike many adults, Robby is not ashamed to bow his head and pray in public. He can get loud as he prays, too. One night, as we ate at a restaurant, Robby led the family blessing so loud that the people at nearby tables turned around to see what was going on.

I can't tell you all the words that he says in the

blessings; but I'm sure God knows, and that's what counts the most.

Dear God, I find that my faith is increased by my praying child. May you always keep words of gratitude and praise for you on my child's lips.

———

Meditate on Ecclesiastes 3:1-8.

Besides becoming a mother, nothing has ever been more thrilling to me than becoming an aunt for the first time. I will never forget how precious my new niece looked when I saw her through the glass of the hospital nursery. I stood at that glass with tears pouring down my cheeks. I was so happy, so proud—and this brand new gift from God was my niece! I recently watched that "baby" walk into her new high school for the first time, and I wondered how she could be so grown when it seemed like only weeks ago when she was born.

Now I look at my two toddlers playing with their toy cars. Tomorrow you'll be driving cars of your own. Today you have to be helped up and down the front steps of our house, but tomorrow you'll own your own homes. You don't know how to read yet, but tomorrow you'll be writing me letters from college. Time passes so quickly. I am thankful for the time we have now to play, for tomorrow you will be grown.

O God, time goes so quickly. My babies will not be babies very long. I have so much to teach them, and they have so much to teach me! Please help me to realize what a precious time we have together right now. Help me to slow down, to listen, to enjoy them, and to savor this time while they are little.

———

Meditate on Thessalonians 5:17-18.

The other day I sent Allison to the bathroom to wash her face. Allison trotted toward the bathroom to carry out her task—or so I thought. Five minutes later she came to me with a pencil and paper asking me to help her write a letter to her grandmother. Seeing that her face had not been touched, I refocused her attention and sent her back to the bathroom. Five more minutes passed, and I heard her singing in the bathroom. When I saw her with a still dirty face, I reminded her that her current job was not to sing but to clean. Yet another five minutes passed, and I found my dirty-faced daughter in her room hosting a tea party for her doll. As I led her to the bathroom she explained, "There are so many things to do that I keep on forgetting what I'm supposed to do."

Many of us have the attention span of a five-year-old when it comes to praying. The other day as

I sat down to pray, I was distracted by the thought that I needed to defrost the chicken we were having for dinner. Then I remembered that the next day it was my turn to provide preschool snacks. By the time I got back to my prayer, the baby was demanding to be fed.

It takes discipline and practice to develop a rich prayer life. I have found that having a prayer partner helps me to be more disciplined in my prayers. Some of my friends say that praying out loud or praying in the shower helps them stay focused on their task. Another busy mother keeps a pad and pen handy as she prays and simply jots down the distracting thoughts that invade her prayers, promising to attend to them at a more appropriate time.

The methods we employ to help us deal with our distractions are not important. What is important is that we find ways to spend quality time in developing a closer relationship with God.

O God, be patient with me as I try to find ways to overcome the distractions that interrupt my time alone with you.

Meditate on 1 Samuel 1:19-28.

Some close friends of mine recently adopted a new baby girl. What an exciting time! The baby is so tiny and sweet, and she has been welcomed into a home where all hopes for ever having a child were nearly gone.

After trying for some time to get pregnant, my friends had to wait a long time to be accepted by an adoption agency. Then they had to wait until the agency found a baby for them. But now their home is filled with joy and happiness, and I doubt that that child could have found a more loving set of parents!

It must have been difficult for the birth mother to give up her child. I think of Hannah, who had promised God that if she could give birth to a child she would let him grow up in the Temple and serve God all of his life. She did have a baby, Samuel, and she let him grow up under the care of a priest, Eli.

As difficult as it was, Hannah gave her baby into the care of Eli and then sang a song to God. She knew that sometimes God has a plan for children to grow up with parents other than their natural parents, and she trusted God.

I hope the birth mother of my friends' baby knows that God took care of her baby and found loving parents for her, just as God took care of Hannah's Samuel.

O God, I pray for birth mothers everywhere who feel it is best to give their babies up for adoption. May their hearts be full of songs of joy and peace, and may they rest knowing that you have found loving parents for their babies.

———

24

Meditate on Matthew 4:19.

One day last fall our neighbors took our children on their first fishing trip. When they returned from their expedition a few hours later, my daughter's face beamed with excitement as she showed me her catch—a fifteen-inch catfish. My son was excited, too, as he told me about the little fish that he caught but had to throw back in the water so it could grow some more. My children's faces were filled with sheer joy as they told me over and over of their afternoon of fishing. I delighted in their enthusiasm and excitement.

Jesus told those who followed him that they were to become fishers of people, casting their nets with enthusiasm and drawing in people to hear about the exciting good news that he had to offer. Today we need to recapture the excitement of catching that first fish as we witness our faith to others. We need to recapture the enthusiasm of children as we tell people over and over again the stories that changed our lives and can change their lives, too. As fishers of people, we need to regain the sense of anticipation as we experience the sheer joy of sharing the good news.

O God, help me witness my faith to others with childlike enthusiasm.

———

25

Meditate on Ephesians 6:1-5.

Most of the time I am happy and content in my role as a mother, but I admit there are days when I am so low I could just sit and cry. The things that get me low are things like having to pick up toys for the hundredth time, having to change a dirty diaper—again—and having a child hang on my leg while I am trying to walk across the room.

Now, to anyone except a mother, these things sound insignificant and maybe even funny. I admit it often is hard to find sympathy. That is why I am glad that I have friends with young children. They know just what I am talking about when I have had enough! They "bear my burdens," and I bear theirs. There is nothing like a good friend, especially when a glass of milk has been tipped over—again!

O God, thank you for the friends I have who understand my situation. They lift me up, and I pray that I may lift them up when they need it, as well.

———

26

Meditate on Psalm 139:13-16.

One afternoon meeting hit a boring and tedious stretch. My eyelids felt like weights, and my mind wandered from the printed agenda before me. The reality that I was pregnant added some legitimacy to my lethargy.

Drowsiness threatened to overtake me, when all of a sudden I felt a fury of tiny taps from within my slightly extended tummy. I'd been anxiously awaiting these first fetal movements. They brought joy and excitement to me and turned that boring meeting into an all-important occasion.

My head was no longer drooping. My eyes were wide open, and there was a smile on my face. Something got ahold of me; it was the feeling of a brand new life. I had felt the movements during my first pregnancy, but once again there was something new and exciting about me—and God was responsible for it. The first kicks energized me because they confirmed the reality that I was carrying a living, breathing person. From then on, how could anything be boring?

Dear God, I praise you for the opportunity to carry a life within my body. Make me a worthy vessel of this young life.

27

Meditate on Psalm 27:14.

Hello?" I whispered sleepily into the telephone. "Mom," a hesitant twenty-three-year-old voice responded, sending me into bolt-upright terror; "I've had a bicycle accident."

For nine months we wait, and it is an apt rehearsal for what lies ahead: more waiting—for first teeth, first words, first steps, and a good night's rest as we forever sleep with one eye open and one ear to the ground.

Waiting is a long tradition of mothers. Moses' mother waited at home while her daughter waited in the bulrushes to see which way the tides would flow for the infant boy. Mary waited in a stable, in a temple, and on a hillside.

Mothers of inventors, artists, and pioneers wait to see which will greet their offspring: applause or jeers. Mothers of soldiers wait for the 6:00 P.M. news. Mothers of outlaws wait in courts. Mothers of ill children wait by bedsides. Mothers of starving children wait for food.

Mothers of all children: We are a sisterhood of waiting. And when a midnight call comes, all the waitings are "kaleidoscoped" into moments when waiting reaped good news, and we dare hope: Christmases, birthdays, report cards, proms, colleges, jobs, mates.

The prayer came unbidden as I waited to hear the next words over my husband's questions and my own thundering heartbeat, *"Dear God, wait with me."*

"Mom," the voice continued, "I'll be okay. I'm at the hospital waiting for the doctor to sew up a few places on my face."

"Hold on," I replied, leaping into action, "we'll come wait with you."

Lord, be with us in our times of waiting, and strengthen and sustain us with your reassuring presence.

28

Meditate on Psalm 78:2-4.

Tell us that story again, Mommy," the children begged. I had just finished telling them the same story for the third time, and yet they wanted to hear it again. My children never seem to tire of listening to stories. Although they enjoy books, they are especially fond of the stories I make up. Most of the stories I tell are about situations that are familiar to them—lost kittens, birthday parties, chipmunk families, and little boys and girls going on outings to the park. The children relate my stories to themselves and become personally involved in the outcomes.

Jesus was well aware of the powerful nature of storytelling. The stories he told, although they were about ordinary people and events, captured his listeners' attention and fed their hunger for a new way of living in the world. Those who listened and heard went home transformed. Those who listened but did not hear went home angry.

Jesus' stories are well worth retelling to ourselves and to our children. The more we tell them, the more we become personally involved with the characters and the outcomes, and the more we open ourselves up to their transforming power.

O God, help me be open to your transforming power, and enable me to be a good storyteller so that my children also may be open to the transforming power of Jesus' stories.

29

Meditate on Ephesians 4:11-13.

I don't remember exactly when my daughter began to talk. All I know is that over a period of about two years her coos became babbles, her babbles became syllables, her syllables became words, and her words became sentences. By the time she was two years old, her speech was fluent and complex.

On the other hand, my son's speech developed in a totally different manner. When he was two and a half years old, his speech was so limited that the pediatrician referred him to a speech therapist for further evaluation. Then one day he suddenly spoke in full sentences, and he hasn't stopped talking since!

Faith development is as varied and individual as speech development. Because I was born into a Christian home and attended church every Sunday, my faith journey has been gradual and fairly steady.

I can identify several important milestones in the development of my faith, but I cannot pinpoint the exact time and place that I first believed in God through Christ. In contrast, a friend of mine had a dramatic conversion experience several years ago, and she is able to point to the precise moment that her faith was born.

It matters not how or when our faith journey began. The important thing is that we allow our faith in God through Christ to guide us through life's journey, to give us strength when we are troubled, to challenge us when we stray, and to remind us of God's constant presence in our lives.

Gracious God, guide me as I continue to grow in faith and to nurture the faith development of my children.

———

30

Meditate on Luke 10:38-42.

Remember playing doggy and kitty?" they asked each other.

I do.

I'd supplied them with towels for beds and food and water to "lap" from bowls on the floor. We still call corned beef hash "dog food."

It wasn't exactly listening at keyholes, but the effect was the same: I was eavesdropping on my grown-up kids' conversation instead of cleaning the kitchen, having shooed aside their offers to help. Together for my fiftieth birthday, they were "remembering when." Backyard circuses, doll hospitals, truck stops, inventions, books—their lists, as their play had been, were endless.

In none of these freeze-framed memories, though, is there a tally of dust bunnies, dirty dishes, or my other housekeeping failures. For I, too, enjoyed playing.

The life we live today is tomorrow's home movie. What images will I want flickering across memory's screen? The clean kitchen that—once again—was trying to take me from communion with this trio? Or heads bent close together in laughter, conversation, play?

"Hey, Mom, are we having 'dog food' for supper?" they hollered. Once again laying aside a dishrag, I yielded to temptation and joined them, giving my answer in person.

Lord, remind us that we can clean an empty house later. Keep us in the picture today; clean kitchens don't rate star billing.

———

31

Meditate on Exodus 19:4-5.

It was a wonderful fall day. It was cool, but the sun was shining; and there was just the touch of a light breeze. I was pushing my children in their swings. Back and forth, back and forth. And each time I pushed, they yelled, "Higher, Mommy!" They laughed and giggled. They were as free as birds, flying higher and higher through the air.

The Bible says, "I bore you on eagles' wings. . . . Now therefore, if you obey my voice and keep my covenant, you shall be my treasured possession out of all the peoples" (Exodus 19:4-5). Wouldn't it be wonderful if my children stayed so close to God all their lives that they felt as free and empowered as they do soaring on the swings? I wonder why I feel so down and out a lot of the time. I wonder why I often don't feel that I am really soaring on the eagles' wings I have been promised. Perhaps I stray too far from God. Perhaps I need to listen more closely to God's voice. Perhaps I need to swing more often—to remember what soaring on eagles' wings feels like.

O God, help me stop feeling burdened with life and instead fly with you as my guide. And perhaps if you and I show my children what flying on eagles' wings is like, they, too, will spend their entire lives soaring with you.

———